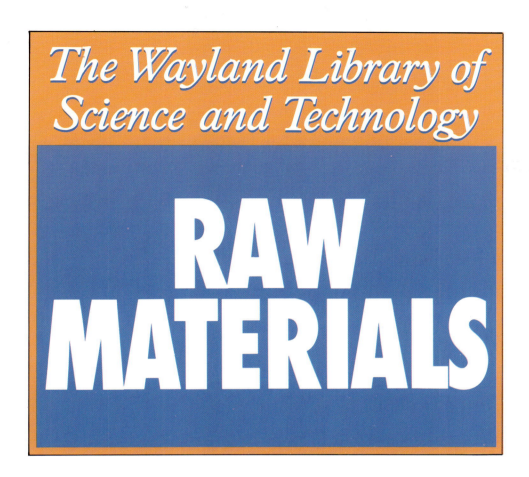

ROBIN KERROD

The Wayland Library of Science and Technology

The Nature of Matter
The Universal Forces
Stars and Galaxies
The Solar System
The Changing Landscape
Air and Oceans
Origins of Life
The Science of Life
Plants and Animals
Animal Behaviour
The Human Machine
Health and Medicine

The Environment
Feeding the World
Raw Materials
Manufacturing Industry
Energy Sources
The Power Generators
Transport
Space Travel
Communications
The Computer Age
Scientific Instruments
Towards Tomorrow

Advisory Series Editor
Robin Kerrod

Consultant
Dr. J. Beynon

Editor: Caroline Sheldrick
Design: Cooper-Wilson
Picture Research: Alison Renney
Production: Steve Elliott
Art Director: John Ridgeway
Project Director: Lawrence Clarke

First published in 1990 by
Wayland (Publishers) Ltd
61 Western Road, Hove
East Sussex BN3 1JD, England

AN EQUINOX BOOK

Planned and produced by:
Equinox (Oxford) Limited
Musterlin House, Jordan Hill Road,
Oxford OX2 8DP

Copyright © Equinox (Oxford) Ltd 1990

All rights reserved. No part of this publication may be reproduced or utilized in any form or by any means, electronic or mechanical, including photocopying, recording, or by any information storage and retrieval system, without permission in writing from the publisher and copyright holder.

British Library Cataloguing in Publication Data
Raw materials.
 1. Natural resources
 I. Title
 333.7

ISBN 0-7502-0023-5

Media conversion and typesetting by Peter MacDonald, Vanessa Hersey and Una Macnamara
Origination by Hong Kong Reprohouse Co Ltd
Printed in Italy by Rotolito Lombarda S.p.A., Milan
Bound in France by AGM

Front cover: Timber stacked in a woodpile for use as fuel.
Back cover: An offshore drilling installation showing a semisubmersible rig, a gravity-base production platform and a loading buoy with a tanker and storage vessel.

Contents

INTRODUCTION 5

EARTH'S RESOURCES 6
Mineral resources • Metallic minerals •
Non-metallic minerals • Prospecting • The oceans •
The air • The forest

MINING 18
Placer mining • Opencast mining •
Underground mining • Other extraction methods

MINERAL PROCESSING 26
Smelting the ore • Iron into steel • Producing other
metals • Metals and alloys • Ceramics • Glass

SYNTHETICS 36
The pioneers • Refining the crude • Petrochemicals
• Composites

GLOSSARY 44

INDEX 46

FURTHER READING AND PICTURE CREDITS 48

Introduction

The early periods of history are named after the main materials people used for tools, utensils, implements and weapons. Prehistoric peoples lived in a Stone Age. Their tools did not advance much until, in about 3500 BC, they discovered how to smelt ores to make bronze, and they entered a Bronze Age. About 2,000 years later, they began producing iron, and an Iron Age began. In the mid-1800s the Steel Age began.

Steel is still the dominant metal today. Modern technology also uses dozens of other metals for thousands of different purposes. It also uses many non-metallic materials – sand, salt, wood and oil – as raw materials for manufacturing.

Most of the raw materials for making metals and manufacturing are taken from the ground as minerals. This book looks at these raw materials and the methods we use to mine and process them.

◀ Wood is one of the most useful and versatile materials. It is used as fuel, in building, and is pulped to make paper and other products. It also goes to make products such as rayon and Cellophane.

Earth's resources

Spot facts

- In 1869 an almost pure gold nugget weighing over 70 kg was found at Moliagul, in the state of Victoria, Australia. It was named the Welcome Stranger.

- The largest diamond ever found weighed more than half a kilogram. It was discovered in Pretoria, South Africa, in 1905 and named the Cullinan. A gem called the Star of Africa was cut from it, and is now in the Royal Sceptre of the British Crown Jewels.

- The oceans of the world hold some 1,350 million cubic metres of water and contain enough salt to cover Europe to a depth of 5 km.

- A forest the size of Sweden must be cut down every year to supply the world with paper.

▶ Amid dramatic scenery in Utah, USA, oil geologists are boring into the ground with drilling equipment during a seismic survey. In the borehole they will place an explosive charge. They will then record the shock waves from the explosion after they have been reflected from the underground rocks.

Industry uses vast amounts of materials to produce the things we use in our everyday lives. These materials are in turn made from basic substances we call raw materials, which come from the land, the sea and even the air. They form part of the Earth's natural resources. The most useful industrial materials by far are the metals, particularly iron and steel. We obtain metals by processing certain minerals, which we extract from the rocks. Other minerals are processed into chemicals for industry or used as they are. The forests represent another natural resource, yielding timber for construction and for making into chemicals and plastics.

Mineral resources

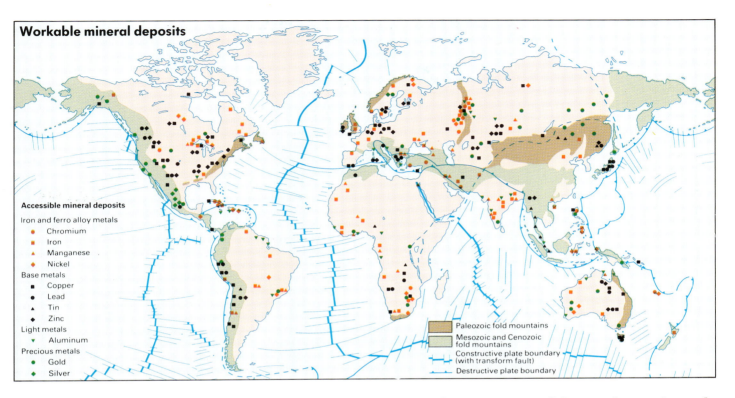

Workable mineral deposits

Accessible mineral deposits
Iron and ferro alloy metals
- Chromium
- Iron
- Manganese
- Nickel

Base metals
- Copper
- Lead
- Tin
- Zinc

Light metals
- Aluminum

Precious metals
- Gold
- Silver

- Paleozoic fold mountains
- Mesozoic and Cenozoic fold mountains
- Constructive plate boundary (with transform fault)
- Destructive plate boundary

▼ Scrapped cars waiting to be recycled. Recycling metals helps to conserve our precious mineral resources.

The Earth's crust, its solid outer layer, is made up of many kinds of rock. Every rock is made up of one or more minerals. Minerals are chemical compounds in which two or more elements are bonded together. Most minerals are made up of a metal combined with one or more non-metals. For example, in the mineral cuprite, copper is combined with oxygen; in galena, lead is combined with sulphur. Copper and lead are metals; oxygen and sulphur are not.

The metal can be extracted from many of the minerals by simple chemical processing. However, it is only worthwhile doing where there are richer, or more concentrated deposits of the minerals, known as ores.

The term "mineral resources" usually refers to those minerals found in ore deposits, which can be profitably worked to produce metals. The map above shows where in the world such deposits are to be found.

Note that ore deposits are not scattered evenly over the globe. They occur in regions where particular geological processes have been at work within the Earth. Many are found in regions where there are fold mountains, at the edges of some of the plates, or segments, that make up the Earth's crust.

7

Metallic minerals

People began using metals about 10,000 years ago. Copper, gold and silver were the first metals to be used because they could be found native, or in metal form in the ground. But they were rare and were used mainly for making trinkets and jewellery. Some fine gold and silver jewellery has been recovered from ancient tombs in the Middle East. It is as beautiful as the day it was made, thousands of years ago.

The reason why gold and silver can be found native and keep their beauty over a long period is that they are not very reactive chemically. In other words, they do not readily combine with other chemical elements. They do not oxidize, or rust, in the way that iron does, for example.

Sometimes huge lumps, or nuggets, of native metals are found. Mostly, however, silver and gold are present in the rocks in specks. They become worth mining only when they have been concentrated into richer ore deposits.

Another important native metal, more precious than gold, is platinum. It is used in jewellery, and also in industry as a catalyst, a substance that speeds up chemical reactions. Platinum is usually found mixed with other metals, including palladium and osmium.

▶ A fascinating variety of copperware displayed in a French town. Copper is easily shaped by hammering.

◀ Gold leaf on the State Capitol in Boston, USA.

▼ Below, a small nugget of native gold.

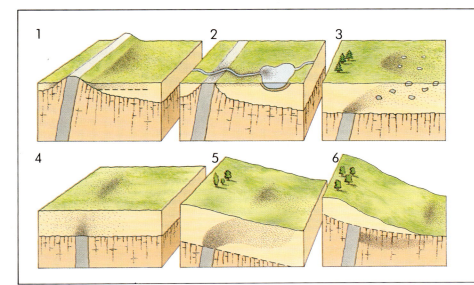

Mineral dispersion

Natural processes can scatter minerals over a wide area. The prevailing wind removes particles from an exposed vein (1). A river running through a vein carries particles away and deposits them downstream in the river bed (2). Glaciers may also erode and transport mineral deposits a long way from the vein (3). The action of water in the soil can break up and scatter minerals (4). So can the creep of soil down a slope (5), and the downward flow of groundwater (6) which can carry minerals away.

Ore minerals

Most metals are too reactive chemically to be found native in the rocks. They occur instead, combined with other elements, as minerals. When we can extract metals from them, we call them ores.

Many ores are oxides, in which the metal is combined with oxygen. Most iron ores, such as magnetite, are oxides. The aluminium ore bauxite is an oxide. Also common are sulphide ores, in which the metal is combined with sulphur. The lead ore galena and the zinc ore blende are both sulphides. The copper ores azurite and malachite are carbonates, the metal being combined with carbon and oxygen.

How ore deposits form

Various natural processes take place in the Earth's crust that concentrate minerals into workable ore deposits. For example, when molten rock, or magma, slowly cools down deep underground, heavy minerals such as iron and chromium oxides tend to settle out first. The large magnetite deposits in Kiruna, Sweden, were formed in this way.

As the magma gradually becomes solid, a hot watery liquid remains which contains various minerals. This liquid works its way into cracks in the surrounding rocks and deposits the minerals as it cools. Such rich mineral veins, or lodes, are widely mined for such metals as copper, lead, zinc and gold.

Other mineral deposits are formed as a result of processes which happen at the surface. Wind, rain and frost slowly break down the rocks and free the minerals they contain. These may dissolve in rainwater and be carried by rivers into the sea. Sometimes sulphur compounds produced by decaying vegetation act on the dissolved matter and produce deposits of sulphides. The copper sulphide ores of Zambia, in Africa, were formed in this way.

▼ A well-shaped crystal of galena, the main ore of lead. It is the chemical compound lead sulphide. Like many metallic minerals, it has a metallic lustre, or shine. The main deposits of galena are found in North and South America, Australia, Spain and Germany.

Non-metallic minerals

Non-metals as well as metals can occur native in the Earth's crust. The chemical elements sulphur and carbon are examples. Sulphur fumes are given out by volcanoes. Vivid yellow deposits of sulphur can often be found around volcanic vents. Most sulphur, however, comes from processing pyrites, the mineral iron sulphide. Sulphur is a vital raw material for industry. It is made into sulphuric acid, one of the most widely used of all industrial chemicals.

Carbon appears in two quite different physical forms in nature. It occurs as black graphite, which is one of the softest of all minerals. It also occurs, more rarely, as transparent diamond. Diamond is the hardest of all minerals. When they are expertly cut, diamonds have a unique brilliance and sparkle, which makes them the most prized of all gems. Diamonds that are of too poor quality for gems are in demand in industry. Their extreme hardness makes them invaluable for grinding, polishing and drilling work.

The most common non-metallic mineral is quartz. Indeed, it is the most common mineral of all in the Earth's crust. It is a form of silica, or silicon dioxide. It is present in many rocks, such as granite, and it is the mineral which, finely divided, makes sand. Sand is used to make concrete, and also in glassmaking.

When quartz is very pure and transparent, it is called rock crystal. When attractively tinted, it forms gemstones, such as rose quartz and amethyst. Pearly opal is another precious form of silica, highly valued as a gem.

Sapphire and ruby are two other precious stones. They are rare forms of the mineral corundum, which is an oxide of aluminium. This mineral contains metal, but it is classed as a non-metallic mineral because its use does not depend on the presence of the metal.

In a similar way calcite, a mineral form of calcium carbonate, is classed as non-metallic. Calcite is found in large quantities in limestone and chalk rocks. Limestone has long been used as building stone. It is also used on a vast scale to make cement.

Most limestones were formed when seas containing dissolved calcium carbonate dried up, or evaporated. Such deposits are known as evaporites. Deposits of rock salt, sodium chloride, were formed in a similar way. Chalk has quite a different origin. It started life as dissolved calcium carbonate in the sea. It was taken out by microscopic organisms to build their chalky skeletons. When the organisms died, their skeletons built up over millions of years to form the thick chalk beds we find today. Such deposits are termed biogenic.

◀ The Pyramids at Ghiza, in Egypt, are built of limestone blocks. The Great Pyramid of Khufu, completed in about 2580 BC, is made up of over 2 million blocks. Some weigh as much as 15 tonnes. It is thought that several thousand workers toiled for 30 years or more on its construction. Limestone is a common building stone, which can be cut readily. In modern cities limestone buildings are being attacked by acid rain.

Rock suits

When firefighters move in to tackle a very hot fire, they wear fireproof suits made of rock. These suits are made from cloth woven from asbestos fibres.

Asbestos is the name given to various silicate minerals that form fibres. The most important of them are chrysolite and crocidolite. More than four million tonnes of asbestos are produced on average every year. Canada and Russia are the world's biggest producers. Asbestos is extracted at surface, or opencast mines.

Less than a third of the asbestos mined has fibres long enough to spin into yarn for making cloth. The rest is used, mixed with other materials, to make building materials and lagging for insulating boilers. Asbestos is mixed with cement, for example, to make pipes and roofing sheets. Its use in buildings, however, is now restricted because asbestos dust poses a health hazard. It causes a disease of the lungs called asbestosis.

▲ This hollow stone, called a geode, was found in Mexico. Millions of years ago a hot mineral-rich solution crystallized inside it, and this is the attractive result. Around the outside is blue agate. Inside are crystals of a purple-tinted variety of quartz called amethyst. Agate and quartz are different mineral forms of the chemical compound silica, or silicon dioxide. Both agate and amethyst are prized as gemstones.

◀ The Big Hole at Kimberley in South Africa. It was once the site of a rich diamond mine. The diamonds were found embedded in a carrot-shaped mass of heavy igneous rock formed from the Earth's upper mantle. It is called kimberlite, or blue ground.

Prospecting

Deposits of minerals are scattered far and wide throughout the world. Looking for mineral deposits is called prospecting. In the past many deposits were found by chance. Others were found by geologists, looking in likely places for particular rocks they knew by experience might contain valuable minerals. Most of these obvious deposits of minerals have now been found and exploited. Most undiscovered deposits lie hidden beneath the surface rocks. Much more scientific methods of prospecting now have to be used to find them.

One of the first stages in prospecting these days is to examine images of the ground taken by satellites. These are called remote-sensing satellites because they carry sensors, or detectors, which look at the Earth's surface remotely, or from a distance. They can "see" not only in visible light, but also in light of other wavelengths such as infrared. At these other wavelengths they can often spot details of the landscape invisible in ordinary light.

Studying satellite images helps geologists select suitable areas to explore on the ground. They carry out tests with a variety of instruments to try to locate the kinds of rocks in which they think minerals might be found. They use such instruments as magnetometers, gravity meters and Geiger counters.

Magnetometers measure the strength of a magnetic field. They indicate changes caused by the presence of mineral deposits, particularly those of magnetic iron ores, such as magnetite. Gravity meters detect slight changes in the Earth's gravity. This might indicate the presence of minerals with a different density from the surrounding rocks. Geiger counters pick up the radiation given out by radioactive substances. They are used when prospecting for the ores of radioactive metals such as uranium.

Geologists also take samples of rock and soil to analyse in the laboratory. This again may give them some clues about where mineral deposits can be found. They take samples from the surface and also drill deep into the rocks to get core samples. The large-scale structure of the underground rocks is investigated by means of a seismic survey.

▼ A Landsat image of Zimbabwe, in Africa, reveals the geology of the region. Landsat is a remote-sensing satellite, which takes pictures of the ground in light of different wavelengths. From the pictures, geologists are sometimes able to locate new mineral deposits.

A seismic survey

In a seismic survey, geologists set up vibrations in the ground called shock waves. Either they make an explosion or they use equipment that pounds the surface. As the waves travel downwards, the rock layers refract (bend) or reflect them. The refracted or reflected waves travel back to the surface, where they are detected by sensitive instruments called geophones. From the way the waves are refracted or reflected, geologists can discover the structure of the rocks.

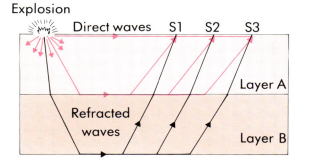

◀ These vehicles are used in seismic surveys. They are fitted with equipment that sets up vibrations in the ground. This method causes much less disturbance than using explosions.

A geological survey

When searching for underground deposits of minerals, geologists first study existing maps and reports about a likely-looking area (1). Then they look at aerial photographs (2) and satellite images which may enable them to pinpoint suitable rock formations. On the ground, geologists sample the rocks (3) and send them for analysis. Seismic testing (4) helps build up a picture of the structure of the underground rocks, while drilling (5) is done to sample them.

1

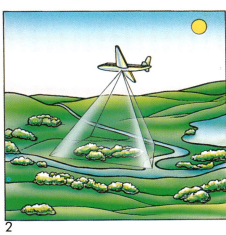
2

3

4

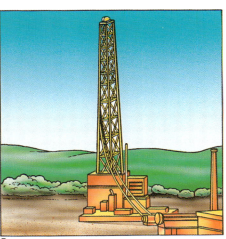
5

The oceans

▲ This desalination plant in Saudi Arabia, in the Middle East, produces fresh water from the sea. It is an expensive process. The word desalination means "removing the salt from".

◀ There are about 35 parts of dissolved substances in every 1,000 parts of seawater. The column (left) shows the relative amounts of the main ones present.

More than two-thirds of the Earth's surface is covered by sea, to an average depth of nearly 4 km. It contains common salt, the chemical sodium chloride. It also contains the salts of many other metals as well. They include the chlorides, sulphates and carbonates of magnesium, potassium and calcium.

The salts that are now dissolved in the sea came originally from rocks on the land. The action of the weather released minerals from the rocks into the rivers, and the rivers then carried them into the sea.

Seawater represents a vast storehouse of raw materials for the chemical industry. Common salt is already extracted from it on a large scale in many countries where the climate is hot. Much of the world's magnesium is obtained from seawater by electrolysis: passing electricity through it. Seawater is also the main source of the element bromine.

On the seabed in many parts of the ocean is another valuable resource, manganese nodules. These are rounded lumps of mineral matter that are rich in the metals manganese, copper, nickel and cobalt. No one is sure about how they form, but they are being produced at the rate of millions of tonnes a year.

The air

The air in the atmosphere is made up of a mixture of gases, mainly nitrogen, oxygen and argon. In every 100 cubic metres of air there are 78 cubic metres of nitrogen, 21 of oxygen and about 1 of the noble gas, argon. In addition there are traces of other noble gases, such as helium, neon, krypton and xenon.

The oxygen in the air takes part in every industrial process involving burning in air. Substances combine with oxygen when they burn. A major use for nitrogen is in the Haber process. This combines nitrogen with hydrogen to produce ammonia, used to make fertilizers and explosives.

Nitrogen and oxygen are also used in liquid form at very low temperatures. Liquid nitrogen (nitrogen at −196°C) is widely used as a freezing agent in industry. Liquid oxygen (−183°C) can be used as an explosive, and is one of the most common rocket propellants.

Liquid nitrogen and liquid oxygen are produced by the distillation of liquid air. Air itself is liquefied by the Linde process, named after the person who developed it. The process involves repeatedly compressing, cooling and expanding the air. On each expansion, the temperature falls. Eventually it falls below the boiling point of air, and the air condenses, or turns into liquid. By carefully distilling the liquid it can be split up into the gases of which it is formed. Distilling liquid air is the main method of producing the noble gases.

▲ This flask is cooled to very low temperatures by liquid nitrogen. It is used to store samples of human sperm. Sperm can be kept in this way for long periods.

▶ The Space Shuttle blasts off the launch pad at the Kennedy Space Center in Florida, USA. The main orbiter engines burn liquid hydrogen and liquid oxygen propellants.

The forest

From the earliest times, the wood from trees has been one of the most useful and versatile materials people have used. It is used as a fuel, and as a material to build houses and make furniture. It has also been used for more than a century to make woodpulp. Most woodpulp is made into paper. Some provides the starting point for a range of other useful materials, such as rayon fibres, Cellophane film and other cellulose products.

Apart from wood, trees produce many other useful substances. These include rubber, which is made from the sap of rubber trees. Solvents for paints can be made from the resin that oozes from the bark of pine trees.

Softwoods

About a third of the Earth's land surface is covered with forests. The two most heavily forested regions are the boreal (northern) forests of the Northern Hemisphere and the tropical rain forests, centred on the Equator.

The boreal forests are made up of conifer trees, which have needle-like leaves and bear their seeds in cones. Most conifers are evergreens, which never lose all their leaves at once. Their timber is generally quite soft and easy to work. For this reason, they are known as softwoods. Firs, pines and spruces are examples. Softwood timber is the main raw material for woodpulp and the construction industry.

Hardwoods

By contrast, the timber from trees of the tropical rain forests is usually hard. For this reason the trees are called hardwoods. Ebony, teak and mahogany are examples. These trees have broad leaves and are never bare, because they lose only a few leaves at a time. In some countries, these trees are protected.

Other kinds of hardwoods grow between the tropical and boreal forest regions. They are made up mainly of deciduous trees: ones that shed all their leaves in the autumn. Examples are ash, oak, birch, beech and sycamore. Tropical and deciduous hardwoods are used for making furniture, flooring and panelling.

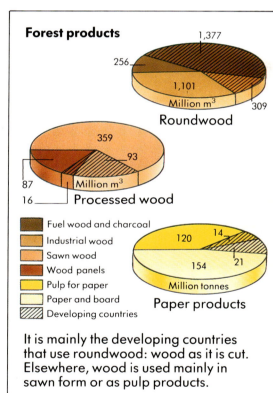

It is mainly the developing countries that use roundwood: wood as it is cut. Elsewhere, wood is used mainly in sawn form or as pulp products.

◀ A timber mill in British Columba, Canada. Logs felled in the surrounding forests are floated to the mill in the form of huge rafts. At the mill, they are sawn into standard lengths and thicknesses for the timber trade. The forest forms part of the great belt of coniferous, or evergreen forest that girdles the Northern Hemisphere. Most of the trees, such as spruces (inset), have a conical shape. This helps them shed snow better.

▲ A forest scientist tends seedlings at a tree nursery in Ghana, in West Africa. The seedlings have been raised as part of a selective breeding programme to produce trees with more desirable characteristics, such as faster growth, a better yield of timber and more resistance to disease. The seedlings will be transplanted to plots in the forest. The seeds of the best trees will then be used in further experiments.

Mining

Spot facts

- The Western Deep Levels gold mine in South Africa is the world's deepest mine, with shafts extending down nearly 4 km below the surface.

- The temperature at the lowest point in the Western Deep Levels mine is 55°C, far hotter than in the hottest deserts on the surface.

- The Bingham Canyon copper mine, near Salt Lake City, Utah, USA, is the world's largest opencast mine. It covers an area of over 7 square kilometres and has been excavated to a depth of nearly 800 metres.

- More than 10 million tonnes of salt are extracted from seawater by evaporation every year.

Our early ancestors began digging materials from the ground in prehistoric times. So mining can be considered the earliest industry. Prehistoric people mined for flint to make tools. Mining became more important about 6,000 years ago when we learned how to extract metals from ores in order to make tools. As the need for materials, especially metals, grew, so mining activities expanded. Today something like 50,000 million tonnes of materials are removed from the Earth's crust by mining every year. Seven out of every ten tonnes comes from surface, or opencast mines. The rest is extracted from underground mines or by using specialist methods, such as evaporating seawater. As natural resources become scarcer, we are having to mine in ever more remote areas.

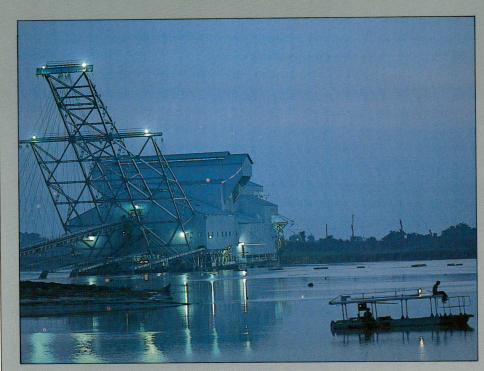

▶ This huge dredger removes cassiterite from an artificial lagoon in Malaysia, in South-East Asia. Cassiterite is the ore from which tin is produced. It is found in large quantities around the Malay Peninsula.

Placer mining

In regions where the rocks contain gold, particles of the metal in time become dislodged under the action of the weather. Streams wash them away, but they eventually settle out in the stream bed because they are so heavy. They form deposits known as placers.

During the great "gold rushes" of the 1800s in California, Canada and Australia, people made fortunes by mining gold in placer deposits. The traditional method of doing this was panning: swirling around the gravel in a pan. The swirling action let any gold particles separate out and fall to the bottom. Further swirling then washed away the light, unwanted gravel, leaving the heavy gold "dust" behind.

When working on a larger scale, miners washed the gravel through troughs called sluice boxes. These were lined with sheep fleeces or felt, which trapped the gold dust as it settled out. A similar method is still used in some gold-mining areas. Miners use a water gun (a "hydraulic giant") to break up gold-bearing gravel and wash it into troughs. Here, grooved devices called riffles trap the gold.

Dredging
On a very much larger scale still, gold is extracted from stream beds by dredging. This method is also used widely to mine cassiterite, or tin ore. This ore is unusually heavy, which makes it possible to mine by placer methods.

The dredgers used for mining in water are great floating ore-processing plants, which can handle as much as 15,000 tonnes of gravel a day. The most common type is the bucket dredger. It has digging buckets in an endless chain mounted on a boom, which angles down into the water to reach the gravel bed.

The mined materials are sieved, or screened, and the finer material is washed over riffles, where the heavy ore or metal settles out. The unwanted material passes through the dredger and is usually dumped on the bank as spoil.

A great deal of gold is also mined underground. Over the years the spoil from the mines has built up into huge dumps. Because extraction methods have improved, these spoil dumps have now become a valuable source of gold.

▲ A miner in north-west Pakistan searches for gold in a river bed using a traditional method, a variation on panning. He pours a mixture of gravel and water on to a makeshift sieve. Particles of gold are washed into the pan underneath, where they settle out because they are heavier than the other mineral matter.

▶ A huge dump of spoil, or waste, at a South African gold mine. The spoil was discarded during early and less efficient mining operations and still contains a significant amount of gold which could not be recovered at the time. It is now a major source of the metal. High-pressure hoses are used to break it up and wash it into processing plants, which dissolve out the gold by treatment with cyanide.

Opencast mining

Mineral ores are easiest to mine when they lie on or near the surface of the ground. Then they are extracted by the opencast, or open-pit method. Minerals mined in this way include iron ores, bauxite (aluminium ore), some copper ores and asbestos.

Opencast mines are by far the largest mines. At the huge Bingham Canyon copper mine in Utah, USA, some 90,000 tonnes of ore are mined each day. Some 3,500 million tonnes of material have been removed since it opened.

The overburden
In a typical opencast mine, the ore deposits lie beneath a layer of unwanted soil or rock. This is called the overburden, and has to be stripped away before mining can begin. This is done by huge excavating machines. One is the bucket-wheel excavator, which has a rotating wheel with digging buckets mounted around the edge. Another is the walking dragline, so called because of its unusual method of motion. Some of these machines can cast their digging bucket 100 metres and scoop up more than 50 cubic metres of material at a time.

After the overburden has been removed, the ore body, if it is hard, must be broken up with explosives. Then it is loaded by mechanical shovels into railway wagons or trucks.

Surface deposits of china clay are so soft that they can be broken up by water jets and then washed into treatment plants.

Quarrying building stone

Stone such as limestone, marble and granite has been used for building since the early days of civilization. The Great Pyramids of Egypt, for example, are built of limestone blocks. The famous Taj Mahal at Agra, in northern India, is built of pure white marble. White marble from quarries at Carrara, in Italy (pictured above), was used by the great sculptors Michelangelo and Leonardo da Vinci.

In a quarry workers split the stone carefully using the natural "grain" of the rock. In hard rock such as granite they drill holes in a line and then drive in wedges. In softer rock such as limestone they cut a groove in the stone by machine. Blocks may also be cut by wire saws.

▼ A huge mechanical shovel loads an ore train at the Valdivia nitrate mine in northern Chile, South America. Chile has one of the world's largest deposits of sodium nitrate, otherwise known as Chile saltpetre.

▶ An opencast mine in Colorado, USA, working molybdenite, the main ore of the metal molybdenum. The picture shows the vast scale of opencast operations, which can extend over many square kilometres.

Underground mining

The ores of iron, aluminium and copper, for example, are often found on or near the surface and can be extracted by opencast mining. However, most metal ores are found locked in the rocks underground. Some are found in quite large deposits, others only as relatively thin veins running between the rock layers. The deposits may be horizontal or slope at any angle, following the angle of the rock layers.

A mineral vein may show itself at the surface as an outcrop. But usually it is detected indirectly from geological investigations. These include seismic tests and measurements by such instruments as magnetometers, gravity meters and Geiger counters. If the signs are good, then holes are drilled into the rocks to produce core samples: cylinders that give a cross-section of the rock layers. If ore is reached, it is assessed chemically for its metal content. Geologists then try to work out how far the ore body extends.

The cost of mining

To justify underground mining, there must be enough ore to make it worthwhile. This is because the cost of underground mining is very high compared with that of surface mining. The cost of boring shafts and tunnels is high. So is the cost of making an underground mine into a place safe enough for miners to work.

In a typical mine, a main shaft is sunk vertically into the ground. Then tunnels are dug horizontally out from it at various levels to reach the ore deposit. A lift, or cage, is fitted in the shaft to carry the miners between the surface and the working levels. A hoist, or skip, is also fitted to lift the ore to the surface.

As mining progresses, the tunnels lengthen.

Railways then need to be laid to transport the miners and ore between the shaft and working face. In some mines the ore is transported by conveyors. The world's largest underground mine has a network of tunnels totalling more than 560 km in length. It is the San Manuel copper mine in Arizona, USA.

For safety, the shafts must be lined and the tunnels supported in areas where the rock is weak. Ventilation equipment must be installed to keep the miners supplied with fresh air and to remove dust and potentially dangerous gases. In coal mines in particular, methane gas, often called firedamp, can seep from the rocks. This forms an explosive mixture with air that can be set off by a spark. In particularly deep mines, the air also needs to be refrigerated because the temperature increases with depth.

In underground mining, miners generally use explosives to break up and remove the ore from the rock. First, "shot-holes" are drilled in the rock face to take the explosive charges. Hand-held pneumatic hammer drills, or jackhammers, may be used. They are rather like a roadmender's drill and work by compressed air. Sometimes a number of drills may be mounted on a wheeled frame called a jumbo to drill many holes at once.

The space from which ore is removed is called a stope. Often ore is removed by the room-and-pillar method. Pillars of ore are left here and there during mining to support the roof of the excavation. Later, the pillars themselves may be recovered, allowing the roof to cave in.

Because coal is soft enough to be cut, semi-automatic machines can be used to remove it. Coal is the decayed remains of huge plants that grew hundreds of millions of years ago.

▲ Working in a salt mine in Kewra, Pakistan. Usually, the salt deposit is broken up by explosives and then loaded mechanically into railway wagons for removal. Deposits are often many metres thick.

◄ A miner uses a compressed-air drill to bore a shot-hole in the ore face in an African mine. Electric drills are not used underground because of the danger that sparks will set off any explosive gases present. After drilling, an explosive charge will be placed in the hole and detonated to break up the ore body. The broken rock will then be transported by skip.

▲ A sharp-toothed mechanical shearer slices through the coalface in an underground mine. It travels along the face, ripping out the coal, which is removed by a chain conveyor. The shearer works under the protection of "walking" props. These are metal roof supports that move forward as the coalface is cut back. Water from the cutting head lubricates, cools and lays the dust.

Other extraction methods

Apart from the traditional opencast and underground mining methods, there are others that have been developed to extract particular minerals. For example, the mineral fuel petroleum, or crude oil, is extracted by drilling. Drilling also features in borehole mining, used to extract minerals such as salt and sulphur. The minerals in seawater can be removed by solar evaporation, using the heat of the Sun. Techniques of removing minerals from the deep seabed are also being investigated.

Drilling
Oil is found trapped in the rock layers. It can be detected from the surface by such methods as seismic surveying. It is reached by holes bored by rotary drills. The drilling takes place from drilling rigs about 60 m tall. A drill bit, with rotating cutting wheels, is attached to the end of a drill pipe. The pipe is gripped and turned by a device called the rotary table.

As the bit bores deeper, more and more lengths of pipe have to be added. When the bit has to be changed, the whole string of pipes is withdrawn by the lifting gear high up in the rig. Mud is pumped down through the hollow drill pipes to lubricate the wheels of the bit and to bring back the rock cuttings.

The borehole is usually lined with steel pipes as it deepens. If oil is struck (and often it is not), the hole is capped with a "Christmas tree". This is a complex of valves and tubes, from which the oil can be extracted at a controlled rate.

There is such a demand for oil that deposits are being tapped in the remotest places, such as the bitterly cold Arctic. Offshore drilling is done

▶ (Main picture) An oil drilling rig in the far north of Alaska, where temperatures may plummet to −50°C and below. The floor of the drill rig is enclosed and heated to protect the operators. Oil began to flow in large quantities from the Alaskan oilfields in 1977, when the Trans-Alaskan Pipeline was completed.
(Inset) A close-up of activity on a drilling rig. The drill bit needs changing, and hundreds of metres of pipe have to be extracted first from the borehole.

▲ This chemical plant in Israel extracts salt and other minerals from the water. The seawater is first pumped into large ponds to allow impurities to settle out. Then it passes to crystallization pans, where the water evaporates. Salt and other minerals are deposited.

by drill ships or semisubmersible rigs. The oil is extracted from massive production platforms that rest on or are pinned by piles to the seabed.

Borehole mining

Traditionally, the mining of rock salt takes place by normal underground mining methods. But at many salt mines these days the salt is extracted differently. A hole is drilled down to the underground deposit, and then water is pumped in. The salt dissolves in the water to form a strong solution of brine. Then the brine is pumped back to the surface. The water is then evaporated off by heating, and the salt separates out.

Sulphur is mined by a similar method, called the Frasch process after the man who developed it. This process uses three pipes of different diameters, one inside the other. Water is heated above its boiling point and pumped down into the deposit through the outer and middle pipes. This causes the sulphur to melt.

Then after about a day, the supply of water to the middle pipe is stopped, and air is forced at high pressure down the inner pipe. This forces a frothy mixture of molten sulphur and hot water up through the middle pipe to the surface. The mixture goes into settling tanks, where the sulphur settles out nearly 100 per cent pure.

Deep-water mining

Many valuable minerals and metals, including common salt, potash and magnesium, are extracted from seawater by evaporation or electrolysis. Other valuable minerals are present on the deep seabed in the form of manganese nodules. They can be mined using a suction method. Further development awaits new technologies and international agreements over the mining rights to such deposits.

Mineral processing

Spot facts

- About 600 million tonnes of iron and steel are produced every year in the world, nearly 50 times as much as aluminium, the next most useful metal.

- A blast furnace operates continuously for months at a time, and can produce 8,000 tonnes or more of pig iron every 24 hours.

- Deadly cyanide poison is often used to extract gold from its ores.

- Several tonnes of some uranium ores have to be processed to produce a kilogram of the metal.

▶ Red-hot molten steel pouring from a converter at a steelworks. It takes only about three-quarters of an hour for a converter-full of pig iron from a blast furnace to be refined into steel.

A few minerals, such as diamonds and native gold, can be used more or less as they are dug from the ground. But the majority of minerals need to be processed in some way before we can use them. Most mineral ores, for example, have to be heated to high temperatures in a furnace before they yield metals. Metals can be extracted from some ores by passing electricity through them. Furnace methods are also used to process many non-metallic minerals. Limestone, sand and clay, for example, are burned, or "fired", to produce a wide range of ceramic products, such as pottery, bricks and cement.

Smelting the ore

A common method of extracting metals from their ores is by heating them in a furnace to high temperatures. This process is called smelting. Iron, for example, is made by smelting iron ore in a blast furnace.

Most iron ores are oxides, in which the iron is combined with oxygen. The main object of smelting is to remove this oxygen. Any earthy impurities in the ore must also be removed.

Iron ore is loaded, or charged, into the furnace with coke and limestone. The coke burns and heats the furnace to a temperature of up to 1,600°C. It also reacts chemically with the iron ore. Coke is mainly carbon, and it combines with the oxygen in the ore to form carbon monoxide gas, which escapes. The iron is left behind. Because of the high temperature, it is molten. It trickles down and collects in the base of the furnace, or hearth.

Meanwhile, the earthy impurities in the ore combine with the added limestone. They form a liquid called slag. This too runs down to the hearth and settles as a layer on top of the molten iron. From time to time the furnace is opened, or tapped, to extract the slag and iron.

Years ago the molten iron ran into a trough and from there into small moulds. These moulds were called pigs, since they were side by side like piglets feeding from a sow. The iron became known as pig iron, and the term is still used. Today, however, most pig iron is fed into huge travelling ladles, which carry it directly to the steelmaking furnaces. In these furnaces the iron is further purified, or refined.

Blast furnaces are also used to smelt other metals, including lead. Lead ore cannot be smelted as it is because it is a sulphide: the metal is combined with sulphur. First it has to be roasted in air. This changes it to an oxide, which the furnace can handle.

Most ores contain a good deal of earth and rock, called gangue. As much of this as possible must be removed before smelting. Methods of removing the gangue, and concentrating the ore, are known as mineral dressing. They use differences in such properties as density or magnetism to separate the ore from the gangue. Flotation is one useful method.

▼ Steel scrap on a quayside in Florida. Large amounts of steel scrap are added with pig iron to steelmaking furnaces. The scrap is carefully selected, so that the resulting steel will have the right composition.

Flotation

In this method of mineral dressing, the earthy ores are finely crushed and fed into a bath of water, to which an oil or chemical has been added. When air is bubbled through the bath, particles of ore attach themselves to the bubbles and form a scum on top. This is then skimmed off. Earthy particles remain behind.

Iron into steel

Pig iron is produced when iron ore is smelted with coke and limestone in a blast furnace. It is not pure iron, but contains a lot of impurities, particularly carbon (about 4 per cent). This makes the iron brittle. Only when most of the carbon is removed does the metal become really useful. It then becomes steel.

Steel is the name we give to the alloy, or mixture, of iron with traces of carbon. The presence of just a few parts per thousand of carbon makes iron much stronger and harder than it is when pure.

In steelmaking, the excess carbon is literally burned out of the pig iron in a furnace. Most steel is now made by the basic-oxygen method. The carbon burns off when a jet of oxygen is blasted into the molten pig iron. The highest quality steel is made by melting selected steel scrap in an electric-arc furnace. Heat is produced in this furnace by an electric arc: a kind of continuous electric spark.

Steelworks are vast. They not only produce the metal, but also carry out many shaping processes, such as rolling, forging and casting.

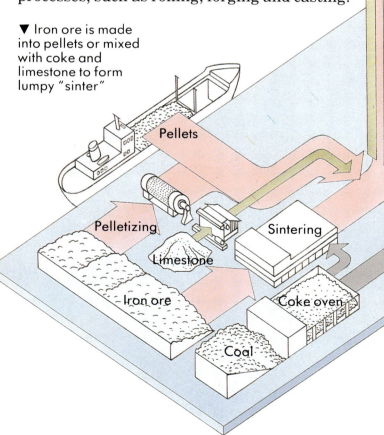

▼ Iron ore is made into pellets or mixed with coke and limestone to form lumpy "sinter"

▼ Steel scrap is usually added to the furnace. Other metals which may be added are nickel, manganese, and chromium.

▲ The blast furnace is a steel tower, standing about 60 m high and measuring 10 m in diameter. Iron ore, coke and limestone are charged into the top of the furnace through a "double-bell" valve system. This prevents the loss of the furnace gases, which include carbon monoxide. The gases are burned as fuel in stoves. These stoves heat the air which is blasted into the base of the furnace.

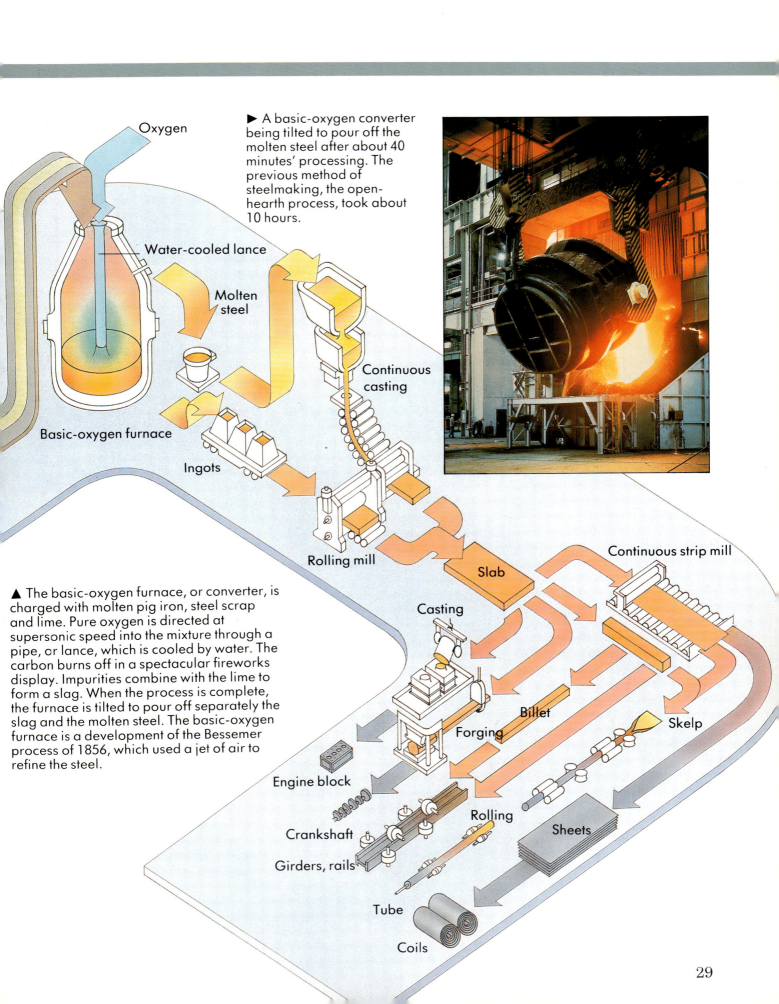

▶ A basic-oxygen converter being tilted to pour off the molten steel after about 40 minutes' processing. The previous method of steelmaking, the open-hearth process, took about 10 hours.

▲ The basic-oxygen furnace, or converter, is charged with molten pig iron, steel scrap and lime. Pure oxygen is directed at supersonic speed into the mixture through a pipe, or lance, which is cooled by water. The carbon burns off in a spectacular fireworks display. Impurities combine with the lime to form a slag. When the process is complete, the furnace is tilted to pour off separately the slag and the molten steel. The basic-oxygen furnace is a development of the Bessemer process of 1856, which used a jet of air to refine the steel.

Producing other metals

Lead, zinc and tin are smelted in blast furnaces in a similar way to iron. Some metals are produced in different kinds of furnaces. Others are extracted by means of electrolysis: this is known as electrometallurgy. Electrolysis is also widely used for purifying metals that may have been extracted by other methods. The extraction of copper from different ores provides a good illustration of these alternative methods.

Copper smelting

Copper often occurs in sulphide ores, in which it is combined with other metals, particularly iron and nickel. The presence of these other metals complicates the extraction process. The following smelting processes are used for the ore chalcopyrite, or copper pyrites, which is a mixed sulphide of copper and iron.

The ore is first concentrated by flotation and then smelted in a reverberatory furnace. Flames shoot over the concentrate and turn it into a bubbling, boiling mass. Some of the iron ore and the earthy impurities together form a slag, which is run off. What remains is matte, a mixture of copper and iron sulphides.

The matte is transferred to another furnace, called a converter, and air is blown through it. Sand (silica) is added, which absorbs the iron and other impurities. This results in blister copper metal, which is about 98 per cent pure.

Smelting aluminium

Aluminium is produced by the electrolysis of molten aluminium oxide. The principle is simple, but the practice is complicated. First, the aluminium oxide must be extracted from bauxite, the ore of aluminium.

This is done by the Bayer process, in which the bauxite is digested with caustic soda (sodium hydroxide). The aluminium oxide dissolves to form sodium aluminate. Crystals of aluminium hydroxide form when the aluminate is cooled. These are filtered off and then heated. This process (calcination) produces alumina (aluminium oxide).

Alumina by itself does not melt until it reaches about 2,000°C. Mixed with a mineral called cryolite, it will melt at only about 1,000°C. In aluminium smelting, a mixture of alumina and cryolite is charged into the furnace. In the furnace, carbon rods (the anodes) are lowered into the molten mixture. Electricity passes between them and the carbon furnace lining (the cathode). The electricity splits up the aluminium oxide into aluminium metal, which collects as a molten layer on the floor of the furnace. Oxygen combines with the carbon anodes to form carbon monoxide, which is led off.

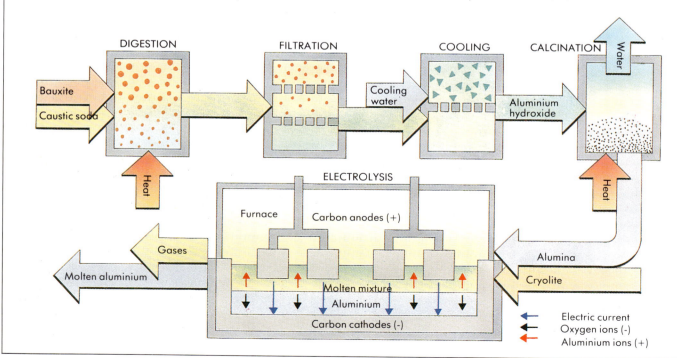

Electrolysis

The purification of the copper is completed by electrolysis: passing electricity through a solution. The impure copper is made into blocks, which become the anodes (positive electrodes) in the process. Sheets of pure copper become the cathodes (negative electrodes). They are placed in a bath of copper sulphate solution, and an electric current is passed through them.

Under the influence of the electricity, copper from the impure anode goes into solution as ions (charged atoms). Pure copper comes out of solution at the cathode, where copper ions change back into atoms. The result is that the anodes dissolve away, while the cathodes grow. Impurities settle out as a slime.

Leaching

The electrolysis of copper sulphate also features in the extraction of copper from oxide ores, such as cuprite. The ores are treated with sulphuric acid, which dissolves the copper as copper sulphate. This kind of process is called leaching. It is an example of hydrometallurgy, the extraction of metals by means of chemical solutions.

Leaching is also an important method of removing uranium, gold and silver from low-grade ores, which contain only the minutest amounts of metal. Uranium is also extracted by treatment with sulphuric acid. Gold and silver are removed from their ores using a weak solution of sodium cyanide.

▲ Molten zinc being tapped from a furnace. Zinc is smelted in a blast furnace, which it leaves as a vapour because of its quite low melting point. Molten metal forms when the vapour is cooled.

▼ The copper in some ores is removed by treatment with sulphuric acid (left). The copper sulphate that forms is then reduced to copper metal by electrolysis. Copper is deposited on the cathode plates of the electrolytic bath (below), which holds the copper sulphate solution. It is deposited as very pure copper.

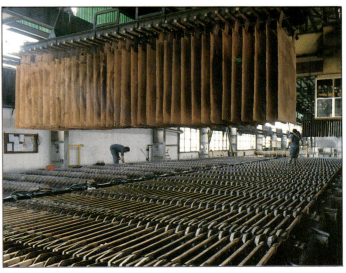

Metals and alloys

Altogether in nature, there exist about 90 chemical elements, which are the basic "building blocks" of matter. Seventy of them are metals. The metals we are most familiar with, such as iron and steel, aluminium, copper and nickel, are tough, strong and quite dense substances. But not all metals are like this. The metal sodium is so soft that it can be cut with a knife. The metal mercury is a liquid at ordinary temperatures. Mercury is the silvery liquid you can see in some thermometers.

All these metals are shiny and pass on, or conduct, heat and electricity well. But we cannot define a metal in this way because some non-metals (such as arsenic) look metallic and others (such as carbon) conduct electricity well.

The scientist defines a metal as an element which, in solution, forms ions with a positive electric charge. Ions are atoms which have lost or gained electrons. The only non-metal that forms positive ions in solution is hydrogen.

Metal properties

Every metal has individual properties that set it apart from the others. For example, iron is magnetic and rusts, or corrodes, easily in moist air. Gold is not magnetic and never corrodes, keeping its shiny appearance century after century. It is not attacked by acids, as other metals are. Only a mixture of concentrated nitric and hydrochloric acids will attack it.

Lead is very soft at ordinary temperatures. Chromium is very hard. Aluminium softens in temperatures of a few hundred degrees. Tungsten will not soften until the temperature rises to several thousand degrees. Cast iron is very brittle and snaps easily. Copper, however, can be bent double without snapping. Copper can also be stretched into a fine wire nearly as thin as a hair without breaking. We say it is a very ductile metal. Gold can be hammered into a very thin sheet without breaking up. We say it is very malleable.

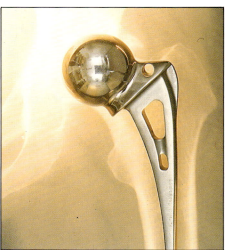

▲ This artificial hip joint is made from titanium and a chromium-cobalt alloy. It is immensely strong and, what is very important, it does not react with body tissues. Stainless steel is another alloy used for implants.

◄ Engineers checking out a turbofan engine. Jet engines are constructed of special alloys that keep their strength at high temperatures. They contain such metals as titanium, nickel and tungsten.

▲ A graceful bronze statue in a public garden in southern England. Bronze is easy to cast in moulds because it flows easily when molten. Bronze does not readily corrode in damp conditions, and so it is an ideal material for outdoor statues and monuments.

Strange as it may seem, most metals are not used in our everyday world in their pure form. In general, pure metals are too weak and too soft to be of use in industry. However, the properties of a metal can often be greatly improved by adding to it traces of another metal or non-metal. Soft and weak iron, for example, is transformed by the addition of traces of carbon into the hard, strong metal we call steel. The weak metals copper and zinc become the strong metal brass when they are mixed.

Steel and brass are metal mixtures we call alloys. Most metals are used in the form of alloys, which are almost always stronger and harder than the metals they are made from.

Metals are also alloyed to improve their chemical properties. Nickel and chromium are metals that do not corrode. When they are added to steel, which by itself does rust, they make the steel rustproof too. The resulting alloy is stainless steel, one of our most widely used alloys. Nickel and chromium are also the main alloying elements in the heat-resistant nichrome series of alloys used in jet engines. One very interesting nickel-iron alloy is called invar. Unlike other metals, it scarcely expands or contracts at all when heated or cooled.

Copper is used in a wide variety of alloys. With tin, it makes bronze; with nickel, it makes cupronickel. Both alloys are used for coinage. Small traces of copper and other metals are added to aluminium. This soft, weak metal is transformed into an alloy as strong as steel, yet only one-third as dense. This alloy, called Duralumin, is almost always used in building aircraft, which must be as light as possible.

Ceramics

Clay was one of the first natural materials used on a large scale. People began using it to make pottery at least 9,000 years ago. They shaped moist clay into pots, bowls and other vessels. Then they baked them hard, first in an open fire and later in a special oven, or kiln.

Pottery is produced in much the same way today, although industrially the process is on a vast scale. It is the most familar example of ceramics. Ceramics are products made by baking clay or other earthy materials in a kiln or furnace. Bricks, cement, glass and refractories are other examples.

Pottery

The ordinary kind of pottery we use every day is called earthenware. It is made from cheap clays and is baked, or fired, at a relatively low temperature (about 1,000°C). It is dull and porous in texture and lets water through. To make it waterproof, it has to be glazed.

The finest pottery, porcelain, is made from pure white china clay. It is fired at a high temperature (about 1,400°C), whereupon it becomes almost glass-like, and waterproof. Porcelain is used widely in the electrical industry because it is an excellent insulator.

Cement and concrete

Cement binds the ingredients of concrete together. It is made by roasting such materials as clay and chalk or limestone at a temperature of about 1,400°C in a rotating kiln. The raw materials are fed to the kiln in the form of a slurry, a mixture with water, or as a moist "cake". Lumps called clinker emerge from the kiln. Dust carried away in the fumes is removed by a precipitator and returned to the clinker. Materials such as gypsum may then be added, and the whole mixture is then ground finely in a rotating ball mill.

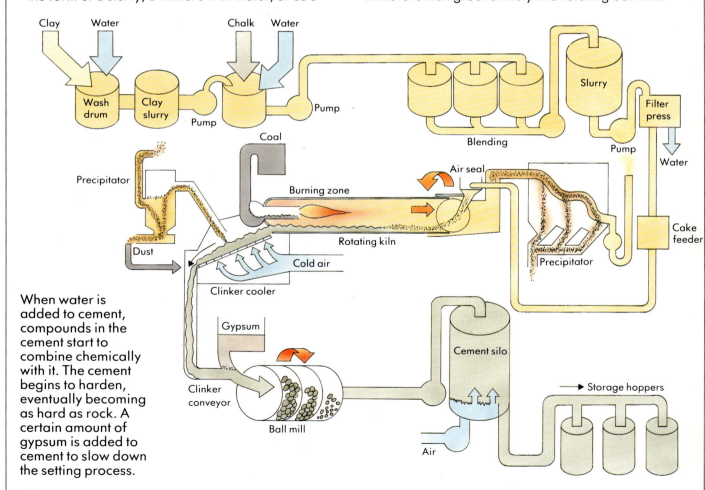

When water is added to cement, compounds in the cement start to combine chemically with it. The cement begins to harden, eventually becoming as hard as rock. A certain amount of gypsum is added to cement to slow down the setting process.

Glass

Stained glass

The art of producing stained-glass windows has been practised for centuries. Some of the most exquisite examples are to be seen in medieval cathedrals in Europe. Stained-glass pictures are made up of pieces of coloured glass, mounted in a lead framework. An artist paints details on the glass with coloured enamels.

Glass is a ceramic product made, not from clay, but from another common material: sand. To make glass, sand is heated in a furnace with a material called a flux, which helps the mixture melt. This happens at a temperature of about 1,500°C. When the molten mass cools and sets hard, it becomes transparent glass.

Ordinary window glass is called soda-lime glass because it is made using a flux of soda ash and lime. These are roasted forms of sodium carbonate and limestone. The heavier and more sparkling glass called lead crystal contains lead oxide. Coloured glasses contain oxides of copper, chromium and other metals.

Refractories

These are substances with exceptional resistance to heat. They are used, for example, to line furnaces and to make pots, or crucibles for melting metals. Refractory materials include aluminium oxide, pure silica (the same mineral as sand) and graphite, a natural form of carbon. Synthetic refractories include tungsten carbide and boron nitride. Tungsten carbide is widely used to make bits for drilling. These bits are able to run red-hot without softening.

◀ Fixing ceramic tiles to a Space Shuttle orbiter. The tiles form the heat shield for the craft, protecting it from frictional heating during re-entry into the atmosphere. Something like 30,000 tiles are fixed to the orbiter, stuck on by adhesive. They are made of pure silica fibre and have the most remarkable insulating properties. They can be red-hot outside but cool enough inside to be touched by the bare hand.

Synthetics

Spot facts

- More than nine-tenths of all organic chemicals used in industry are produced by refining petroleum.

- Every year the United States alone produces 30 million tonnes of plastics, half the tonnage of the nation's wheat crop.

- PTFE, the plastic coating on "non-stick" kitchenware, is as slippery as ice.

- The glass fibres used in glass-reinforced plastics have the same tensile strength as high-quality steel.

Many of the products we use today are made from manufactured materials, rather than natural materials. They are artificial, or synthetic. Some, such as synthetic rubber, are designed to imitate materials which occur in nature. Others, such as nylon and PVC, have no natural counterpart.

Plastics are far the commonest group of synthetic materials we use. They now rank alongside iron, wood and concrete as the most important materials of our age. Plastics are made mainly from petrochemicals: chemicals obtained by refining oil, or petroleum. Petrochemicals are also the starting point for many other products, including drugs, dyes, paints and insecticides.

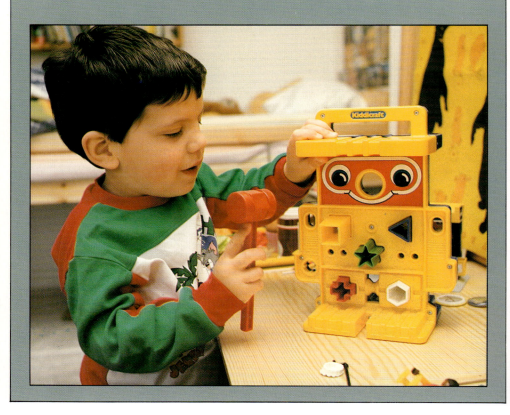

▶ Plastics, the most widespread synthetics, are popular materials for making toys. They can take a lot of knocks without breaking. They keep their colour, because the plastic is coloured all the way through. No harm comes to children who chew them, because they are non-toxic.

The pioneers

The first successful plastic was made in 1870 by the American inventor John W. Hyatt. He was searching for a substitute for ivory to make billiard balls. The plastic he invented was celluloid. He made it by treating the cellulose in wood with nitric and sulphuric acids. This produced nitrocellulose, a material that by itself is too brittle to be useful. Hyatt made it into a useful product by adding a little camphor to it. This made it flexible.

We call celluloid a man-made, rather than a synthetic material. Its starting point is a natural material, cellulose, which is then processed. It was not until 1909 that an American chemist, Leo H. Baekeland, produced the first synthetic plastic, which he made wholly from chemicals. He called it bakelite.

Baekeland was at the time carrying out experiments to find new materials for making varnishes. In his researches he found that the chemicals phenol and formaldehyde (now called methanal) reacted together to form a resinous substance. By controlling the reaction, Baekeland found he made a material that could be moulded by heat. This discovery led to the birth of the plastics industry.

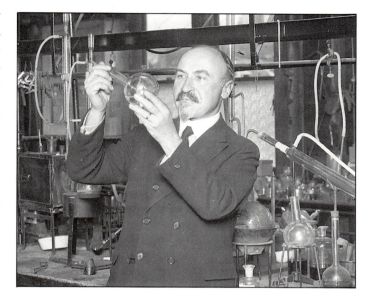

▲ The inventor of bakelite, Leo H. Baekeland, at work in his laboratory. A chemist by profession, Baekeland was born in Belgium. He emigrated to the United States in 1899, at the age of 36.

▼ These desk-top items made from bakelite date from the 1940s. Bakelite became widely available in the 1920s. In the early days it was often used, as here, for making luxury goods.

Refining the crude

When Baekeland made the first synthetic plastic, bakelite, one of the raw materials was phenol. This was obtained from coal tar, then the most important source of raw materials for the newly emerging organic chemical industry.

Coal tar was then produced on a large scale as a by-product in the manufacture of coal gas. It contained a mixture of hydrocarbons: compounds of carbon and hydrogen only. From these compounds, chemists began to make dyes such as mauve, and drugs such as aspirin. They made explosives such as TNT, and eventually plastics such as nylon.

By the 1930s demand for organic chemicals had outstripped the supplies available from coal tar. Producers gradually switched to petroleum as a source instead. Today it is the major source.

Petroleum, or crude oil, is a thick greenish-black liquid, which is made up almost entirely of liquid hydrocarbons. It contains literally thousands of them. But it only becomes useful when it is split up into different parts, or fractions, containing hydrocarbons having a similar boiling point.

The splitting up is done by distillation, also called fractionation. This process is a standard method for separating liquids with different boiling points. First the crude oil is heated in a

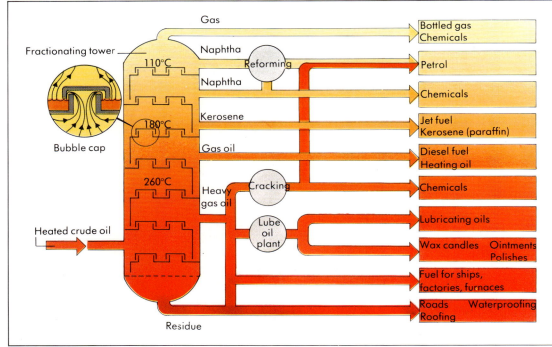

Fractionation

Crude oil is split up into its fractions in a fractionating tower. The hydrocarbons in oil vapour separate out at different levels according to their boiling point. Some hydrocarbon mixtures, such as petrol, can be used more or less as they come from the tower. But most undergo further processing to make them into more desirable products. Some are transformed into chemical raw materials.

▲ Lit up at night, an oil refinery has a strange beauty. It is a huge chemical plant, covering several hundred hectares. The tallest structures are fractionating towers.

▼ Examples of the hydrocarbons found in crude oil. Hexane is a straight-chain compound. Cyclohexane and benzene are ring compounds, with single and double bonds, respectively, between their six carbon atoms.

● Carbon atom
● Hydrogen atom

Hexane

Cyclohexane

Benzene

furnace to a temperature of about 400°C, whereupon much of it turns to vapour. The mixture of hot liquid and vapour is then fed into a fractionating tower up to 80 m high.

Inside, the tower has about 40 perforated trays fixed at different levels across it. Each tray contains liquid hydrocarbons kept at a certain temperature. Temperatures decrease going up the column. Vapour rising up the tower passes through so-called bubble caps, which make it bubble through the liquid in each tray. Each hydrocarbon condenses out of the vapour as it bubbles through the tray kept at a temperature just below its own boiling point.

Many of the fractions obtained by distillation go for further processing. The hydrocarbons they contain are chemically altered to make them into more useful products. Some processes aim to increase the yield of petrol. Others aim to produce raw materials for the organic chemical industry. These are called petrochemicals.

Petrochemicals

The main purpose of petroleum refining has always been to produce fuels, particularly petrol. The initial fractionation of crude oil, however, yields only about one-third petrol, which is the lightest fraction of distillation and the one with the lowest boiling point. Beginning in the 1920s, new methods were developed to improve the petrol yield by processing heavier fractions. These processes are cracking and polymerization.

Breaking down

The most important cracking method requires the use of a catalyst, and is known as catalytic cracking. The object of the cracking operation is to "crack" or split up larger, heavier hydrocarbon molecules into smaller, lighter ones.

The raw material, or feedstock, for cracking is usually the heavy gas oil fraction from the fractionating tower. It is fed into a vessel called a reactor, which is kept at a temperature of about 490°C and at a pressure of two atmospheres (twice normal atmospheric pressure). Inside the reactor, a flow of vapour and air keeps the particles of catalyst suspended in a fluid-like, or fluidized state. This allows intimate mixing of catalyst and vapour and provides ideal conditions for cracking.

The cracked oil vapour is led off to a fractionating tower. From there it goes to other units, which separate out the newly formed lighter hydrocarbons. The most valuable products are naphtha and gases. The naphtha is blended with the petrol fraction.

Building up, rearranging

The gases consist of hydrocarbons with small molecules and a low boiling point which are no use for fuel. So they are now fed to the polymerization unit which builds up the small molecules into bigger ones: the opposite of cracking.

Polymerization takes place at a relatively low temperature (200°C), but at a very high pressure: nearly 70 times normal atmospheric pressure. The result is more hydrocarbons suitable for petrol and others suitable as chemical raw materials.

Another refinery process, called reforming, also improves the petrol yield. It does not break

▼ This diagram shows how chemists fashion a host of synthetic products from a mix of raw materials. These materials are derived not only from petroleum, but also from a variety of other sources as well. These sources include air and natural gas, which is a mixture of light hydrocarbon gases, mainly methane. Limestone (calcium carbonate), salt (sodium chloride) and fluorite (calcium fluoride) are mineral raw materials.

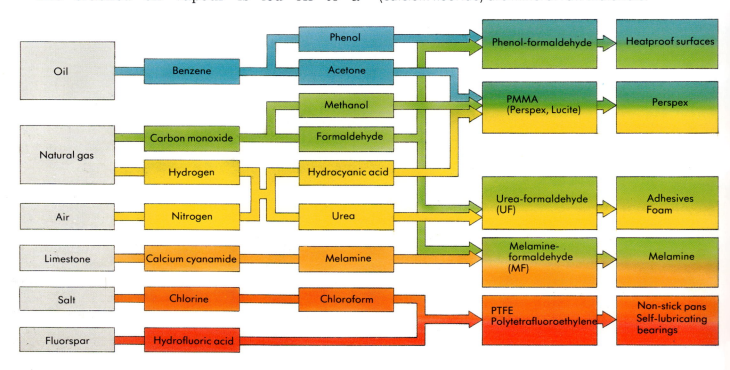

down or build up molecules like the other processes. Rather it rearranges the atoms in the molecules. Reforming is a high-temperature, high-pressure process that requires a catalyst. It uses naphtha as a feedstock and produces a high proportion of aromatics, or benzene compounds. These greatly improve the burning qualities of petrol. Alternatively, the reformed naphtha is available as a source of benzene and other aromatics for the chemical industry.

Petroleum chemicals
Catalytic cracking and reforming are two major refinery processes that produce chemicals as by-products. So does another: steam cracking. Naphtha and gas oil are the main feedstocks for this process. It takes place at a temperature of about 770°C and at atmospheric pressure. Steam is mixed with the feedstock before it enters the cracking furnace.

Steam cracking yields liquids rich in aromatics suitable for petrol. But the most important products are substances called alkenes (or olefins). These are unsaturated hydrocarbons, which means that they contain double or triple bonds between some of their carbon atoms. These double bonds can be easily broken in chemical reactions. In other words, unsaturated hydrocarbons are highly reactive.

By far the most important alkene is ethylene (ethene). It has the chemical formula C_2H_4 or $H_2C=CH_2$, where = means a double bond. The best-known use of ethylene is for making the plastic polyethylene (polyethene) by polymerization. The plastic PVC (polyvinyl chloride) is made by polymerizing vinyl chloride, a chlorine compound of ethylene.

Steam cracking also yields large quantities of propylene (propene), much of which is made into polypropylene and other plastics. Butadiene made into synthetic rubber in combination with styrene.

▼ Petroleum is a vast storehouse of chemical raw materials that has accumulated in the ground over 200 million years or more. Burning petroleum as a fuel in engines and furnaces seems a shameful waste of such a precious asset. The diagram gives an idea of how versatile petroleum is as a raw material. All these things can be made from two tanks full of petrol, which would take a car about 1,000 km.

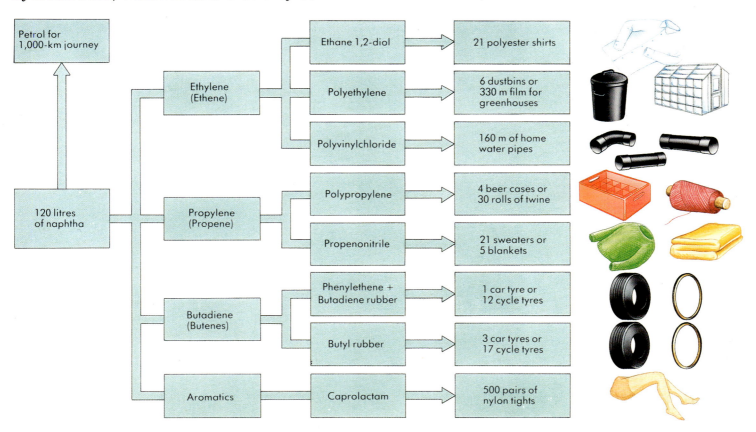

Composites

▲ Many sailing dinghies have their hulls made of fibreglass. Unlike wood, the traditional material for boat hulls, fibreglass resists rotting and is tough enough to resist knocks.

The best pole-vaulters can clear heights of up to 6 m. To achieve such lofty heights, they need to use a pole made from a synthetic material, so flexible that it can bend almost double. This material is fibreglass. It is the most familiar example of a kind of material we call a composite.

Composites are made of a substance, usually plastic, in which fibres are embedded. The fibres reinforce the plastic, and give it extra strength. They tend to stop it cracking when it is put under stress. As well as glass, a number of other kinds of fibres are used in composites, including those made from carbon, refractory materials and metals.

In devising this method of reinforcing with fibres, scientists are copying nature. One of the most remarkable structural materials in nature, bone, is a composite. It is made up of the mineral calcium phosphate, reinforced with fibres of a protein called collagen. This combination makes bone light but very strong.

Glass-reinforced plastics

The correct name for the fibreglass material is glass-reinforced plastic (GRP). Glass fibres may be made in long lengths, or filaments, by melting glass and forcing it through a spinneret. This is a device perforated with hundreds of holes. Alternatively, fibres can be produced in the form of "wool" using a rotating perforated drum. Molten glass introduced into the drum is flung out through the holes by centrifugal force, forming fibres which then break up into short lengths.

Typical GRP products include boat hulls, car bodies and suitcases. These are made by a moulding process. First a mould is made of the required object. Then a mat of glass fibres is laid over it. A synthetic resin (usually polyester) is then poured over the mat. It is mixed with a curing agent, which makes it set into hard plastic. Alternatively, for some products, the glass fibre is chopped very finely and mixed with the resin. This mixture is then sprayed over the mould with a spray gun.

Carbon fibres

Plastics reinforced with carbon fibre have the desirable properties of lightness coupled with strength. They are used in aircraft construction, for example, to make wing and body sections; in medicine to make artificial limbs; and to make sports equipment.

Carbon is unique among the chemical elements in being able to bond strongly with itself to form huge molecules. Most synthetic plastics have such molecules. They are formed of long chains of carbon atoms, to which are attached other atoms (such as hydrogen) or groups of atoms.

Carbon fibres are made by baking plastic fibres, such as acrylics, in an oven. By carefully controlling this process, the side atoms on the molecules can be removed, leaving the very strong long carbon chains. The fibres produced have exceptional stiffness and, weight for weight, have four times the strength of steel.

Fibres similar to carbon fibres can be made from the element boron. But unlike carbon fibres, boron fibres are electrical insulators.

Laminates and cermets

In a broader sense, composites also include a variety of other synthetic constructional materials. They include, for example, plastic laminates. The heatproof working surfaces in kitchens are laminates of synthetic resins, reinforced with paper or cloth.

Cermets are combinations of ceramics and metals, for example, aluminium oxide and chromium. They are designed to combine the heat resistance of ceramics with the strength and machinability of metals. They are widely used for making components for the high-temperature parts of jet and rocket engines.

▼ In making a helicopter blade from GRP, glass fibres have been wound around a mould. Liquid resin will next be applied, which will set into plastic.

▼ A pole-vaulter accelerates on the run-up to the bar. The fibreglass pole he carries is flexible. It will bend and then spring back to help propel him high into the air.

Glossary

alloy A mixture of metals, or of a metal and a non-metal. Brass is a common alloy, made from copper and zinc.

anode A positive electrode; for example, of an electric cell.

aromatics Organic compounds related to benzene that contain a benzene-ring structure.

asbestos Mineral that occurs naturally in the form of fibres.

bakelite The first synthetic plastic, named after its inventor, Leo H. Baekeland.

biogenic deposits Mineral deposits formed from the remains of once-living organisms.

blast furnace The furnace in which iron and other metals are smelted. It is named for the blast of hot air that makes the furnace burn fiercely.

bottled gas Properly called liquefied petroleum gas, or LPG; gas extracted from natural gas that can be readily liquefied under pressure. It is usually propane or butane.

bronze A most useful alloy, being a mixture of copper and tin. It was the first metal widely used, beginning in about 3500 BC, and ushered in a period of history known as the Bronze Age.

catalyst A substance that increases (or decreases) the rate of a chemical reaction without changing chemically itself.

cathode A negative electrode; for example, in an electric cell. In general it is a source of electrons.

celluloid The first plastic, made from cellulose nitrate, with a little added camphor.

ceramics Materials made by heating earthy substances in a furnace or kiln. Pottery, cement and glass are familiar ceramic products.

cermet A combination of a ceramic and a metal; used for its heat resistance in jet and rocket engines.

coal tar A tarry substance obtained by destructively distilling coal: heating it at high temperatures in the absence of air. It was once the main source of organic chemicals.

composite A synthetic material, consisting usually of a plastic, reinforced with a fibre, such as glass or carbon fibres.

cracking An oil-refinery process in which heavy oil fractions are broken down into lighter, more useful ones. It may be brought about with the help of a catalyst or steam. Steam cracking produces a wide variety of chemical raw materials.

distillation A process in which a liquid is heated until it turns into vapour, which is then condensed back into liquid by cooling. It is a common method of separating and purifying liquids.

ductility A property of a metal that enables it to be drawn out into fine wire without breaking.

electrolysis Splitting up a compound in solution or when molten by passing an electric current through it. It is a useful way of producing or refining some metals, including aluminium and copper.

electrometallurgy Using electrolysis to extract or refine metals.

elements, chemical Simple substances made up of atoms with the same atomic number. They are the building blocks of matter.

evaporites Mineral deposits laid down when salty seas evaporated. Deposits of rock salt and gypsum formed in this way.

fibreglass The common name for a synthetic composite made by reinforcing plastic with glass fibres.

flotation A common method of mineral dressing, used to separate ore particles from earthy impurities. Crushed ore is mixed with a frothing liquid, and the ore particles float to the surface with the bubbles.

fractionation Or fractional distillation; method of distillation which can separate a mixture of liquids (such as crude oil) into various fractions with different boiling points.

gangue The earthy and rocky impurities mined with ore.

gem Or precious stone; a mineral used in jewellery, which is prized for its colour, brilliance or sparkle. Diamond, sapphire, ruby, emerald and opal are among the most sought-after gems.

geode A hollow stone or rock that is lined with well-formed crystals.

GRP Short for glass-reinforced plastic; the proper name for the material we usually call fibreglass.

hardwoods Trees, or the timber from trees, which grow in the rain forests (such as ebony and mahogany) and in temperate regions (such as oak and beech).

hydrocarbon A compound made up of hydrogen and carbon only. Petroleum and natural gas are made up almost entirely of hydrocarbons.

hydrometallurgy Extracting metals from their ores by means of chemical solutions.

inorganic chemistry One of the main branches of chemistry, concerned with the study of the chemical elements and their compounds, except carbon compounds containing hydrogen.

ion An atom that has lost or gained electrons. In general metals lose electrons to form positive ions, or cations; non-metals gain electrons to form negative ions, or anions.

leaching Treating a compound with a chemical solution (often an acid) to extract, for example, the metal it contains.

magma Molten rock.

malleability A property of a metal that enables it to be hammered into thin sheet without breaking.

metal An element that is typically dense, hard, tough and shiny; that conducts heat and electricity well; and that can be hammered into thin sheet or drawn into fine wire without breaking. About three-quarters of the chemical elements are metals, although not all of them have all of the above properties. One, mercury, is a liquid at ordinary temperatures.

metallic mineral One from which a metal can be extracted.

metallurgy The science and technology of metals. Various branches are concerned with the properties of metals, and their extraction, smelting, refining and shaping.

mineral A chemical compound found in the Earth's crust. Every mineral has a definite composition and physical and chemical properties.

mineral dressing Preparation of an ore before smelting. Its main purpose is to concentrate the ore and remove unwanted earthy wastes.

native element An element that is found in a pure state in nature. Gold and carbon are two native elements.

non-metallic mineral A mineral that may or may not contain a metallic element. If it does contain a metal, its use does not depend on there being metal present.

nugget A lump of native metal, such as a nugget of gold.

opencast mining Mining on the surface of the ground.

ore A mineral from which metal can profitably be extracted. Many ores are metal oxides and sulphides.

organic chemistry The branch of chemistry concerned with the study of the wealth of carbon compounds containing hydrogen. Such compounds were originally termed "organic" because it was thought that they could be made only by living organisms.

overburden A layer of soil over an ore deposit near the surface of the ground.

panning A method of mining for gold used by early prospectors, in which they swirled round a mixture of gravel and water in a pan.

petrochemicals Chemicals obtained by processing petroleum in a refinery.

petroleum Or crude oil; a greenish-black liquid obtained by drilling into the ground. It is a mixture of thousands of hydrocarbons, which is separated into useful products by refining.

pig iron Iron produced in a blast furnace. It contains too many impurities to be useful by itself and so is refined, into steel.

placer deposit A deposit of a heavy mineral, such as gold or cassiterite (tin ore), found in stream beds.

plastic A synthetic material made up of long molecules which can be moulded into shape by heat.

polymerization A chemical reaction in which a substance with small molecules (the monomer) is converted into a substance with large molecules (the polymer).

prospecting Looking for mineral deposits.

PTFE The plastic polytetrafluoroethylene, known for its exceptional slipperiness.

quarry A surface mine from which stone, sand or gravel is extracted.

quartz The most common mineral in the Earth's crust. It is a form of silica, the compound silicon dioxide.

recycling Reprocessing used materials so that they can be used again.

refining Purifying or converting materials into a more useful form; for example, petroleum and metals.

refractories Materials that resist high temperatures.

salt A chemical compound formed when an acid reacts with a base. Common salt, sodium chloride, is the most familiar salt.

seismic survey A prospecting method in which geologists set up shock waves in the ground, and then record the way they are reflected and refracted (bent) by underground rock layers.

smelting Heating an ore at high temperature in a furnace in order to reduce it to metal.

softwoods Trees, or the timber from trees, which grow mainly in the cold boreal (northerly) regions of the world. They are typically conifers, such as pines, firs and spruces.

solar evaporation Using the Sun's heat to evaporate water; for example, from seawater in order to extract the salt it contains.

spoil The waste material excavated from a mine along with the ore.

steel The most important metal by far. It is an iron alloy, containing traces of carbon and other metals, such as manganese.

synthetics Materials that are wholly made of chemicals.

vein A gap between rock layers that has become filled with minerals.

Index

Page numbers in *italics* refer to pictures.

A

acid rain 10
Africa 9
air 15
Alaska 24
alkenes 40
alloys 28, 32, 33
alumina 30, 32
aluminium 26
   smelting of 30
amethyst *11*
ammonia 15
argon 15
aromatics 40
asbestos 11, 20
Australia 6, 9, 19
azurite 9

B

Baekeland, Leo 37, *37*
bakelite 37, *37*
basic-oxygen process 29
basic-oxygen converter *29*
Bingham Canyon copper mine 18
blast furnace 26, *26*
blende 9
bricks 34
brine 25
bromide *14*
bromine 14
bronze 33, *33*

C

calcination *30*
calcite 10
calcium *14*
Canada 11, 17, 19
cassiterite 18
Cellophane 16
celluloid 37
cellulose 16, 37
cement 34
ceramic tiles *35*
ceramics 26, 34
cermets 42
chalcopyrite 30
chalk 10
Chile 20
Chile saltpetre 20
china clay 20, 34

chloride *14*
chromium 28, 32
clay 26, 34
coal 23
coalmining *23*
cobalt 14
composites 42-43
conifers 17
copper 8, 9, 14, 32
   extraction of 30, *31*
crude oil 40
cuprite 31
cyanide 19, 26

D

desalination *14*
diamond 6, 10
diesel fuel *38*
distillation 15, 38
dredging *18*, 19
drilling, for oil 24, *24*
drugs 38
Duralumin 33
dyes 38

E

Earth's crust 7
Egypt 10, 20
electric-arc furnace 28
electrolysis 25, 30, 31
electrometallurgy 30
evaporites 10
explosives
   manufacture of 15, 38
   use of 20, 23

F

fertilizers 15
fibreglass 42
firedamp 23
fleeces 19
flotation 27, *27*, 30
fluorite *41*
fractionating tower *38*, 39
fractionation 38
France 8
Frasch process 25

G

galena 7, 9
gangue 27

gases 15
Geiger counter 12, 22
geode *11*
gems 10, 11
geological survey *13*
geology 12, 13, 22
Ghana 17
glass 35
glass-reinforced plastics 36, 42
gold 6, 8, 9, 19, 32
gold leaf *8*
gold, native *8*
"gold rushes" 19
granite 20
graphite 10
gravity meter 12
gypsum 34

H

Haber process 15
hardwoods 17
hip joint, artificial *32*
Hyatt, John 37
hydrocarbons 38, *39*, 40, 41
hydrometallurgy 31

I

India 20
insecticides 36
ions 31, 32
iron 26, 32
   smelting of 27
Israel 25
Italy 20

J

jackhammer 23
jet engine 32, *32*
jet fuel *38*
jewellery 8
jumbo 23

K

kerosene *38*
kimberlite 11

L

laminates 42
leaching 31

lead 9, 32
    smelting of 27, 30
lead crystal 35
limestone 10, 20, 26
Linde process 15

M

magma 9
magnesium 25
magnetite 12
magnetometer 12
malachite 9
Malaysia 18
manganese 28
manganese nodules 14, 25
marble 20
matte 30
mercury 32
metals 7, 32
    native 8, *8*
methane gas 23
methanal 37
Mexico 11
mineral deposits 7
mineral dispersion *9*
minerals 7, 9
    non-metallic 10-11
    processing of 26-29
    prospecting for 11-12
mining 18-23
    borehole 24
    deep-water 25
    opencast 20
    placer 19
    underground 22-23
molybdenum 20

N

naphtha 40
nickel 14, 28, 32
nitrogen 15
nuggets 8
nylon 36

O

oil 24
oil refinery *39*
opencast mining 20, *21*
openpit mining 20
ores 7, 9, 18, 20, 27
    formation of 9
osmium 8
overburden 20

oxidation 8
oxides 9
oxygen 15, 27

P

paints 36
Pakistan 19, 23
palladium 8
panning 19, *19*
paper 6
paperboard *17*
petrochemicals 36, 40-41
petroleum 24, 36, 38, *41*
    refining of 40
phenol 38
pig iron 26, 28
placer mining 19
placers 19
plastics 36
platinum 8
polymerization 40
porcelain 34
potassium *14*
pottery 34
propellants 15
prospecting 12-13
PTFE 36
PVC 36, 41
pyrites 10

Q

quarrying 20
quartz 10

R

rayon 16
refractories 34, 35
resin 16
riffles 19
rolling mill *29*
room-and-pillar method 23
roundwood 17, *17*
rubber 16
rust 8, 32, 33

S

salt 23, 24, 25
sand 10, 26, 30
satellite image *12*
satellites 12
Saudi Arabia 14

seawater 14, 18
    components of *14*
seismic survey 12, *13*
shot-holes *22*, 23
silica 10, 30, 35
silver 8
slag 27, 29
smelting 27
sodium *14*, 32
softwoods 17
South Africa 6, 11, 18, 19
Space Shuttle *15*
stained glass *35*
statue, bronze *33*
steel 26
    scrap *28*
    smelting of 28
Steel Age 5
steelmaking 28
stope 23
strontium *14*
sulphur 24, 25
Sweden 9
synthetics 36-43

T

tin, smelting of 30
titanium 32
tools 5, 18
Trans-Alaskan pipeline 24

U

underground mining 22-23
uranium 12, 26, 31
USA 8, 15, 18, 20, 23, 36

V

volcanoes 10

W

Western Deep Levels mine 18
wood 6, 16
woodpulp 6, 16, 17

Z

Zambia 9
Zimbabwe 12
zinc 9
    smelting of 30, *31*

Further Reading

Bricks by Terry Cash (A. & C. Black, 1989)
Focus on Resources series (Wayland)
The Oil Industry by Malcolm Keir (Batsford, 1988)
The Science of Structures and Materials by Robin Kerrod (Macmillan, 1985)
Rocks, Minerals and Fossils by Keith Lye (Wayland, 1988)
The Earth's Resources by Don Radford (Batsford, 1986)
Rock and Mineral by R. F. Symes (Dorling Kindersley, 1989)
Everyday Chemicals by Kathryn Whyman (Gloucester Press, 1988)

Picture Credits

b=bottom, t=top, l=left, r=right.
BCL Bruce Coleman Ltd, London. GSF Geoscience Features, Ashford, Kent. MARS Military Archive and Research Services, Braceborough. RHPL Robert Harding Picture Library, London. SC Spacecharts, Wiltshire.

4 Zefa/W H Muller. 6 Zefa/McAllister. 7 Robert Estall. 8t, 8bl SC. 8br, 9 GSF. 10 RHPL/W Rawlings. 11t SC. 11b De Beers Consolidated Mines Ltd. 12 Hunting Technical Services Ltd. 13 Larry D Brown/Cornell University. 14 Hutchison Library/T Beddow. 15l Frank Spooner Pictures. 15r SC. 16 BCL/Keith Gunnar. 16-17 RHPL. 17 Holt Studios. 18 Susan Griggs Agency/David Alan Harvey. 19l RHPL/F Jackson. 19r Colorific/Terence Spencer. 20t Zefa/P Freytag. 20b Vautier-Decool. 21 RHPL. 22-3 Hutchison Library. 23l RHPL. 23r National Coal Board. 24-5 Zefa. 24l, 24r SC. 26 Zefa/Helbing. 27l Pasminco Mining. 27r Robin Kerrod. 29 Nippon Steel Corporation. 31t, 31br Rio Tinto Zinc Photo Library. 31bl Colorific/Terence Spencer. 32l SC. 32r Zefa. 33 SC. 35t Sonia Halliday Photos. 35b Rockwell International/MARS. 36 Sally & Richard Greenhill. 37t Brown Brothers. 37b Design Council/Katz Collection. 38-39 Tony Stone Worldwide. 42 John Walmsley. 43l BASF. 43r Zefa.